He Has Risen...

With ALL Power

Produced and Published by Infinite Generations
137 National Plaza, Suite 300
National Harbor, MD 20745
1-(855)-455-0125
www.infinitegenerations.com

ISBN:
978-1-953364-49-4 (Paperback)

Printed in the United States of America
First Printing, 2024

Edited by: India Spruill Howard

Photography from Canva

Power of the Cross
The Path to Redemption

Infinite Generations Publishing
Faith Word Healing Books

Introduction
POWER OF THE CROSS

Palm Sunday is the beginning of Holy Week. Jesus triumphantly rode into Jerusalem on a donkey with His disciples and was met by a crowd who had come to Jerusalem to celebrate the Annual Passover Feast. As Jesus approached, the crowd waved palm branches and shouted, "Hosannah! Hosannah! Blessed is He who comes in the name of the Lord." The crowd was anticipating the Kingdom of God, and Jesus would save them from the Pagan ruler of Israel and build God's true Kingdom. They were expecting Jesus to make a public speech, but instead, Jesus said, "Render to Caesar the things that are Caesar's." That is not what they wanted to hear. The crowd became upset with Jesus and felt they did not need Him. So they decided to charge Him with treasonous pretending to be "King of the Jews."

Jesus knew as He rode into Jerusalem that He would be killed and pay the penalty for our sins so we may have eternal life in God's Kingdom. John 3:16, "For God so loved the world, He gave His only begotten Son, that whosoever believeth in Him should not perish, but have everlasting life." Jesus explained to His disciples that He must go to Jerusalem to suffer, stand trial, and be killed at the hands of the law but rise on the third day. Mark 10:33-34, "Saying, Behold, we go up to Jerusalem; and the Son of man shall be delivered unto the chief priests, and unto the scribes; and they shall condemn him to death, and shall deliver him to the Gentiles: And they shall mock him, and shall scourge him, and shall spit upon him, and shall kill him: and the third day he shall rise again."

Matthew 16:22, "Then Peter took him, and began to rebuke him saying, Be it far from thee, Lord: this shall not be unto thee." It was hard for His disciples to understand why Jesus must be killed. According to scripture, on the night of His arrest, He told His disciples, John 14:6, "Jesus saith unto him, I am the way, the truth, and the life: no man cometh unto the Father but by me." On the day of His trial, TRUTH stood before Pontius Pilate, knowing that the final verdict of His trial would be death. Only through His death on the Cross and rising again on the third day would the penalty for our sins be paid. He went willingly to the Cross so we may have eternal life.

Acknowledgements

This book would not have been possible without the extraordinary people who strongly support me.

First, I thank God for giving me the knowledge to write.

Thanks to my husband, Elijah, who consistently shows patience and understanding while I am writing.

Thanks to my daughter, India, who helps to organize and edit most of my books. She firmly believes the books I write will empower and benefit many people.

Of course, none of this would have been possible without the full support of Infinite Generations Publishers. The team showed faith in helping pull this book together, and I am grateful to them.

Finally, I want to thank everyone who will take the time to read and share this book with others.

Contents

Holy Week Timeline

Holy Monday

Jesus cleanses the temple
Matthew 21:12-19

Wednesday

Judas and Sanherin

prepare to arrest Jesus
Matthew 26:1-16

Palm Sunday

Jesus enters Jerusalem
Matthew 21:1-11

Holy Tuesday

Judas betrays Jesus
Matthew 26:14-16

Maundy Thursday

The Last Supper
Matthew 26:20-75

Easter Sunday

Jesus has risen with all power!
Matthew 28:1-6

Good Friday

Jesus' Crucifixtion
Matthew 27:1-61

Silent Saturday

Jesus lay dead in a

guarded tomb
Matthew 27:66

Palm Sunday

Palm Sunday marks the beginning of Holy Week, symbolizing the entry of Jesus into Jerusalem. Accompanied by His disciples, Jesus rode into the city on a donkey, greeted by a jubilant crowd that had gathered for the Annual Passover Feast.

As Jesus approached, the crowd waved palm branches and exclaimed, "Hosannah! Hosannah! Blessed is He who comes in the name of the Lord." The people were filled with anticipation, envisioning the establishment of the Kingdom of God. They believed that Jesus would liberate them from the rule of the Pagan leader in Israel and usher in God's true Kingdom. Expecting a powerful declaration from Jesus, the crowd's enthusiasm was met with unexpected words: "Render to Caesar the things that are Caesar's." This response contradicted their expectations, leaving the crowd disappointed and dissatisfied. The mood shifted, and the crowd, once hopeful, became upset with Jesus. Feeling that they no longer required His guidance, they took a drastic turn, accusing Him of treason and claiming that He pretended to be the "King of the Jews."

The same crowd that joyously welcomed Jesus on Sunday was now ready, by Friday, to demand His crucifixion.

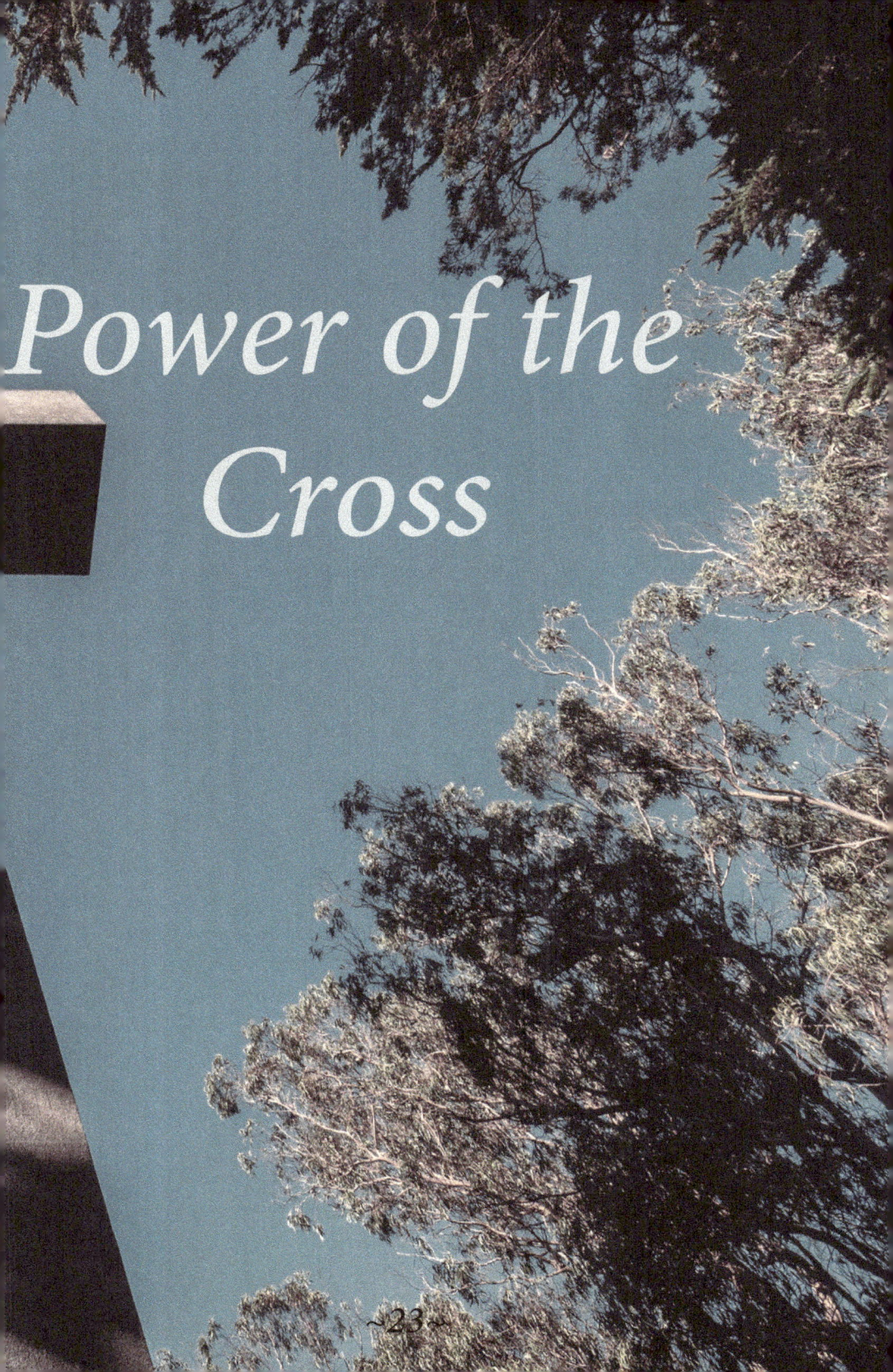

Power of the Cross

"For it is not possible that the blood of bulls and of goats should take away sins."

Hebrews 10:4

During the Old Testament days, sins were not forgiven prior to the cross. Genesis 3:15, tells of God's promise, that the Seed of the woman will conquer Satan. Therefore, the Seed of a woman would bring forth a redeemer, Jesus Christ. Throughout the Old Testament, people believed and kept the faith that ONE DAY their sins would be forgiven.

Today, we BELIEVE our sins are forgiven through Jesus Christ!

Jesus' Seven Sayings from the Cross

Jesus' first words from the cross,

"Father, forgive them;
for they know not what they do."
Luke 23:34

The word encourages us to love and forgive one another. He was falsely condemned, scourged and crucified. Yet, He still prayed for forgiveness for His enemies. During our daily journey, we come up against trials and tribulations as Jesus did. If only everyone would think of how Jesus handled His enemies while yet on the cross, the world would be a better place to live. There would be less stress, blood pressure would be normal and everyone's health would be in perfect control.

His second words from the cross,

"Verily I say unto thee, Today shalt thou be with me in paradise."

Luke 23:43

While hanging on the cross, Jesus continued to show His love and mercy. He would reach out to a man next to Him, who was a criminal and probably never gave any thought to spiritual life. Jesus offered him salvation and eternal life during his last minutes. Today, He continues to offer salvation and eternal life to anyone who will acknowledge and accept His invitation.

***Jesus' third words spoken from the cross
are directed to His mother,***

"Woman, behold thy son!"
John 19:26

Picture Jesus' mother standing there watching as her son hangs from an old wooden cross on Mount Calvary Hill where all the fulfillment of prophecies come together. Yet, she knew that the shedding of His blood was to save mankind. No one can express how Mary felt watching her son bear the burdens of our sins on His shoulders. One can imagine she felt mournful and grateful! Today, we are thankful for Jesus fulfillment of the cross.

The fourth words from the cross,

"My God, my God why hath thou forsaken me?"

Matthew 27:46

When things go wrong in our lives, we find ourselves asking the same question, "why?" We must realize that our Savior has already taken care of the "whys." Our "whys" have been fulfilled by the blood that never loses its power!

Jesus' fifth words from the cross,

"I thirst."

John 19:28

This tells us that Jesus was divine and human. In despair, we should remember our Savior's assurance. He went through everything that mankind would experience while on that Old Rugged Cross.

His sixth words from the cross,

"It is finished!"

John 19:30

As our Savior hung on the cross, His work was finished. He came to seek and save, knowing there was a cross to bear. We can rejoice because the ransom for our sins has already been paid by the shedding of His blood.

His seventh and last words from the cross,

"Father, into thy hands I commend my spirit"

Luke 23:46

Jesus laid down His life for mankind to have eternal life; it was not taken from Him. Yes, Jesus died on the cross and was buried in a borrowed tomb, but wait! The story does not end-- He rose on the third day with all Power! Because He lives, we have the assurance that our journey here on earth has already been worked out!

He Has Risen

His disciples BELIEVED, and today, we BELIEVE our sins are forgiven through Jesus Christ dying on the Cross. On EASTER SUNDAY (RESURRECTION DAY), the third day after His crucifixion, an Angel of the Lord descends and rolls the tomb aside."

"I AM THE WAY, THE TRUTH, AND THE LIFE"

He rose up with ALL POWER!

Heavenly Father,

We pray that this book will be a blessing to all. That your reservoir of anointing will heal every reader and meet their needs. In Jesus name we pray, Amen!

WRITE DOWN WHAT YOU NEED AND MAKE YOUR REQUEST KNOWN UNTO GOD:

_____

_____

_____

_____

_____

_____

_____

_____

_____

_____

_____

_____

_____

_____

SAY, HEAVENLY FATHER, YOUR WORD SAYS, IF WE HAVE FAITH AND BELIEVE, WE SHALL RECEIVE. TODAY, RIGHT NOW, I AM BELIEVING MY CIRCUMSTANCES ARE HEALED. AMEN!

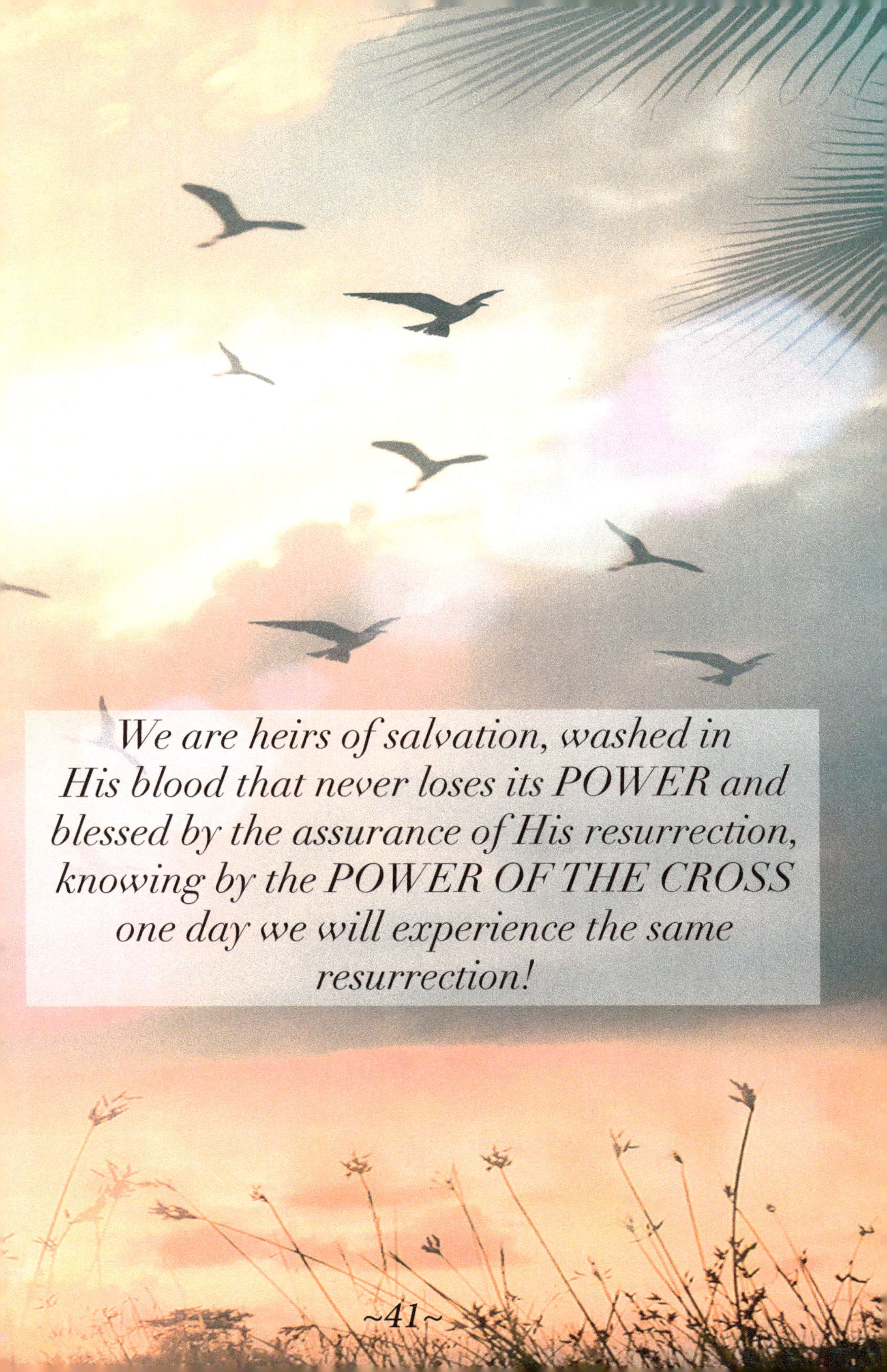

We are heirs of salvation, washed in His blood that never loses its POWER and blessed by the assurance of His resurrection, knowing by the POWER OF THE CROSS one day we will experience the same resurrection!

Thanks for Reading!

Jesus Seven Saying's From the Cross

Luke 23:33-34
Jesus' first words from the cross, "Father, forgive them; for they know not what they do."

Luke 23:43
Second greatest words, "Verily, I say unto thee, Today shalt thou be with me in paradise."

John 19:26-27
His third words spoken from the cross is directly to his mother, "Woman behold thy son!"

Matthew 27:46
The fourth words from the cross, "Eli, Eli lama sabachthani!" meaning, "My God, my God, why hath thou forsaken me?"

John 19:28
Jesus' fifth words from the cross, "I thirst."

John 19:30
His sixth words from the cross, "It is Finished."

Luke 23:46
His seventh and last words from the cross, "Father, into thy hands I commend   spirit: and having se   gave up the gho

Listen to our podcast episode on Jesus Seven Saying's from the Cross

More from
Faith Word Healing

Positive Living Longevity Magazines

A faith-based magazine designed to promote postive living and strengthen your faith!

Available at
Infinitegenerations.com/shop

For more readings to empower your life, check out Faith Word Healing on our website
www.faithwordhealing.org

About The Author

Rev. Dr. Carrie M. Spruill is a dynamic speaker and visionary leader, renowned as the founder of Faith Word Healing Ministries, Faith Word Healing Magazine, Sunday Messages, and Faithful Talk Podcast.

From a young age, Rev. Dr. Spruill exhibited a remarkable gift for teaching and healing, guided by the presence of the Holy Spirit in her life. By the age of twelve, she was already leading adult Sunday school classes, and by sixteen, she delivered her first public speech at a Baptist Convention.

With a passion for biblical studies, Rev. Dr. Spruill pursued extensive education, earning doctoral, master's, and multiple bachelor's degrees. While holding two law degrees in today's world, she notes Jesus' death was twofold. First, His death was an act of God prophesized in the book of (Isaiah, Chapter 53). Secondly, the Roman governor did not believe Jesus was guilty, but out of fear for his position let the people decide to bring charges to crucify Him (Mark 14:43 -72, and Chapter 15). This book gives you a timeline of Jesus' final days on earth.

Drawing from her deep spiritual insight and worldly knowledge, Rev. Dr. Spruill is dedicated to empowering others to fulfill their God-given purposes.

Guided by the belief expressed in Jeremiah 1:5, she endeavors to help individuals recognize and embrace the divine plan mapped out for them before their birth.